MW00623213

BL

THEOLOGY OF

JAMES

by Alvin Shifflett

A Division of Standard Publishing
Cincinnati, Ohio
40009

Library of Congress Catalog Card Number: 74-28724
ISBN: 0-87239-010-1

© 1975
The STANDARD PUBLISHING Company
Cincinnati, Ohio
Printed in U.S.A.

To Trent Sheets

*A young man who wears the blue jeans theology
as prescribed by James*

PREFACE

The letter of James is one of the most practical letters of the New Testament. Luther referred to it as a "right strawy epistle," because he couldn't seem to reconcile James's position of faith. I admire Luther tremendously, but disagree about his estimate of James's letter. There is no straw here, only mortar!

James said: "Faith, if it hath not works, is dead, being alone" (2:17). Paul said: "By grace are ye saved through faith; and that not of yourselves: it is the gift of God" (Ephesians 2:8).

James believed faith could be worn in the blue jeans of works. He felt that Christianity is fit to be lived. His entire letter reflects this blue jeans theology. His advice is practical, sometimes painfully so, and applicable to the shopping malls of life. The man who leaves the assembly of worship on Sunday must carry his beliefs with him on Monday. That is precisely why James wrote: "What doth it profit, my brethren, though a man say he hath faith, and have not works? can faith save him?" (2:14).

As you move through this book I hope you discover, if you haven't already, that the theology of James is tailor-made for you. And the material James uses isn't fancy permanent press double knit, but rough and ready-to-wear blue jeans.

This letter isn't a theological treatise, nor have

I attempted to make it so. But it is theology! I believe James shows us that real theology is to be worn and not left to debate in the hallowed halls of a seminary. Blue jeans theology is to be worn and worn well. If you are looking for ways to apply Christianity, or even better, to wear your Christianity, then here is your pattern: the letter of James.

—*The Author*

CONTENTS

"My brethren, count it all joy when ye fall into divers temptations; knowing this, that the trying of your faith worketh patience." (James 1:2, 3)

PATTERN 1   UNDER FIRE

A Christian farmer had a weather vane on his barn. On it were inscribed the words, "God is love." An ungodly neighbor said in derision, "So God's love is as changeable as the wind?" The farmer replied, "It means to me that God is love no matter which way the wind is blowing!" That is the positive attitude James presents in this letter. The crown of life will be given to all who keep on loving Him, no matter which way the wind blows.

James, the half brother of our Lord, addresses himself to the stormy problem of "keeping the faith" in the midst of trials and tribulations. He is concerned that the believer who comes "under fire" does not change his pattern of faith. I remember an old radio preacher in Virginia who always signed off the air by saying, "Now until next week, remember: keep on keeping on." The old radio preacher knew that the believer would be tried by the fires of tribulation.

The trials of those early Christians probably prompted the writing of this letter. It is perhaps one of the earliest writings of the New Testament era. The church had been scattered by persecution, and there was need for encouragement. The believers were under fire! In Acts 8:1 we read: "And at that time there was a great persecution against the church which was at Jerusalem; and they were all scattered abroad throughout the regions of Judea and Samaria, except the apostles."

So James writes: "To the twelve tribes which are scattered abroad" (1:1). He immediately launches into the necessity of a proper attitude of faith when one is under fire. "My brethren, count it all joy when ye fall into divers temptations" (1:2). In other words, count it joy to be under fire for Christ!

No man is tempted by God. He is tested, but not tempted. Our adversary Satan is the tempter. It is necessary, however, for God to test us. A love that is never tested is a questionable one.

Perhaps we have been responsible in this country for peddling a soft Christianity. We have made our doctrines and theology custom-fit for the comfortably padded pew. We have preached that the church will not go through the tribulation, but will be removed first. Hal Lindsey calls this removal "the Great Snatch," and I subscribe to that. But as a result of this we have inadvertently, and perhaps erroneously, assumed there will be no tribulations. Jesus said: "In the world ye shall have tribulation" (John 16:33), and that is strong medicine.

In this world the believer has to endure suffering and pain, plus a host of other trials. The early church soon discovered the truth of the Lord's statement. Believers behind the iron curtain today know the truth of the Lord's statement. Corrie Ten Boom reveals the Christian under fire in her book, *The Hiding Place.* But in our affluent country we tend to ignore "having tribulations" as not part of the message. We are guilty of presenting a Jesus who always saves or delivers us from the fiery furnace of tribulation. Jesus said: "Lo, I am with you alway even unto the end of the world" (Matthew 28:20), but He didn't imply deliverance on every occasion!

Shadrach, Meshach, and Abednego will testify that "in the world ye shall have tribulation." They were thrown into the fiery furnace for their faith. "Our God whom we serve is able to deliver us from the burning fiery furnace, and he will deliver us out of thine hand, O king. But if not, be it known unto thee, O king, that we will not serve thy gods, nor worship the golden image which thou hast set up" (Daniel 3:17, 18).

They assured the king that God was capable of delivering them from his hands. Notice they said that God *can* deliver, but *may not!* They were thrown into the fiery furnace. God didn't deliver them, but something miraculous happened. The king was astonished and asked: "Did not we cast three men bound into the midst of the fire?" (Daniel 3:24).

Three went in, but four were seen walking around! The fourth had the countenance like a God. I believe it was the Lord himself. He never forgets His own. He was there in the fire with Shadrach, Meshach, and Abednego. He is with us in the fiery furnaces of the twentieth century. The God of Daniel's time is the same God of today. Let us presume His presence and assume His activity.

Everyone likes the Twenty-third Psalm. "He maketh me to lie down in green pastures." That's a very nice picture, a pleasant scene. "He leadeth me beside the still waters." That's even better, quiet and reposeful, tranquillity par excellence! Then we come to that verse of tribulation: "Yea, though I walk through the valley of the shadow of death," and we take trembling steps. But the psalmist claims: "I will fear no evil." How could he not fear?

James probably asked the same question. When the fire comes, and we are thrust into the valley of the shadow of death, fear is overcome with His presence. The Spirit Comforter is here to do just that—comfort, that fear might be overcome with joy. Our three friends in the fiery furnace were not issued asbestos suits. The shield of faith protected them and the presence of God comforted them.

For some reason that doesn't seem to comfort us. We have developed a skillful way in writing off Old Testament miracles as "historical supernatural intervention." Historical is the key word, for we think of it as a thing of the past.

James sees the Christian under fire and stretched to the breaking point. Perhaps the breaking point is our ulceration point. God knows our breaking point. It is the maximum elasticity of our faith. God will never ask us to go beyond this point. He asked that of His Son, but not of us.

Suppose a man hears the gospel and affirms faith in the Lord. He follows the affirmation of faith with baptism. He receives the customary membership and baptism certificates, a new Bible, and a welcome into the fellowship. Shortly afterward he's driving his car on Interstate 70 and the motor conks out. Later, after getting another car, he goes on vacation with his family. They return to find their house has been burglarized. All the furniture has been quietly but quickly removed. Neighbors saw it happening but felt it best to mind their own business. The misfortune of bad luck is that it comes in threes. The man's employer announces that a machine is going to replace him on his job. Automation takes its toll.

The novice cries out, "Lord, what's going on? Hey, it's tougher now than it was before I became a Christian!"

He relates these terrible events to his pastor. "Since I became a Christian my car went defunk, my house was burglarized, and now I'm losing my job. What kind of God do we have? Why didn't you tell me these things would happen?"

The pastor meekly replies, "Well, I meant to tell you there would be trials, but I didn't want to scare you off. You see, I wanted you to join."

"To join!" the man says. "Who wants to join a group that has so many trials?"

The pastor continues, "Well, I was planning to tell you about the trials in new member classes.

You see, James said: 'Count it all joy when ye fall into divers temptations' (1:2)."

There is a possibility that our novice friend will join one of America's fastest growing groups: the Church Obituary Column, better known as the dead membership list.

James is not offering to us some kind of Christian masochistic theology. He isn't suggesting that you rejoice over pain or suffering for suffering's sake. Allow me to illustrate.

I have a toothache and go to the dentist. "Doc, you've got to pull this tooth; it's killing me!" The dentist calmly opens his Bible to the first chapter of James and paraphrases, "Count it all joy when you have such a toothache." He closes his Bible and says, "Now go home and rejoice in your suffering." What would you think of a dentist like that? Is he a religious nut? Does James mean that?

"Doctor," I beg. "Please don't send me away like this. I want my tooth out!"

"Now don't get excited," he urges. "Praise the Lord for the pain."

"Praise the Lord, Doc," I yell, "but pull out my tooth!"

James is certainly not saying what the dentist is suggesting. I have heard Christians, however, suggest such a masochistic theology. *The New International Version* sheds some light on the subject: "Consider it pure joy, my brothers, whenever you face trials of many kinds, because you know that the testing of your faith develops perseverance" (1:2, 3). Notice the connection "trials of many kinds" plus "testing of your faith" produces perseverance.

Your attitude under fire is most important. In Hebrews 12:11 we read: "Now no chastening for the present seemeth to be joyous, but grievous: nevertheless afterward it yieldeth the peaceable fruit of righteousness unto them which are exercised thereby." Consider the same verse rendered from *The New International Version:* "No discipline seems pleasant at the time, but painful. Later on, however, it produces a harvest of righteousness and peace for those who have been trained by it."

My mother-in-law has a great little saying, "This too shall pass." (I think I first heard it in reference to me.) She is saying that with the proper attitude the goodness of future time will overcome and perhaps even erase the badness of present time.

The Christian is to be optimistic, for he is living beyond the present to the future. His is a futuristic life. This is the eternal hope that is within him. No chastening or pain for the present is joyful. We would be foolish and stoic to say so. It is present tribulation! No one can convince me that the Israelites enjoyed their meanderings in the desert for forty years. That was present tribulation. Suppose you had to eat manna every day for forty years. That's tribulation!

Generally we rejoice over escape from tribulation, don't we? It is grievous to go through some trials. If someone were stretching you on the rack, you wouldn't whistle "Dixie." You would probably pray, "Lord, deliver me from this rack and take vengeance on these devils!"

In its proper context, counting it joy under fire suggests an abiding Presence that isn't felt by the non-Christian. A Christian can be at a friend's funeral or even in the hospital himself and still have the confident, calm assurance beneath his grief and pain. It is this confident calm that only God can bring.

Our lives, because of the very fact of our existence, will from time to time be brought into the red zone of danger. Will we have the confident calm of God's presence during our unwilling visit into the red zone?

Our attitude is most essential in the valley of the shadow of death. James is presenting a state of faith that affects the state of mind. You and I both know that there are times when we have a poor attitude, and we make trials, even small ones, practically unbearable. There was such a time in the life of Elijah. Elijah felt all alone and complained to the Lord.

Elijah might have said, "Lord, my circumstances are worse than any other prophet's. Lord, you never allowed a woman like Jezebel to get after other prophets. Give me a stiff-necked Pharaoh, or a stress camping situation of forty years in the wilderness, or confrontation with false prophets, or even prison, but not Jezebel!" Did you ever feel like that?

Your situation is the worst on the block. The Lord told Elijah He had seven thousand faithful, all underground, who hadn't bowed the knee to Balaam. Are we aware of how many Christians are living on our block and haven't bowed the knee to false gods? Probably not, but God is aware of them. We can be confident that even in the worse situations God is with us.

It was during the Civil War that advisers found Abraham Lincoln discouraged over conditions. They suggested, "Cheer up, Mr. President, God is with us."

Lincoln replied, "That's true. But what bothers me is, are we with Him?"

DISCUSSION-STARTER QUESTIONS

1. What is meant by the phrase peddling a soft Christianity? Do you agree?

2. Does Jesus always deliver us from trials? Do we always expect deliverance?

3. What was the popular, yet erroneous concept, held by the new church member?

4. If you had been the pastor, how would you have answered him?

5. What is the red zone of danger? Will everyone have to face a red zone of danger?

6. Is it possible to be joyful under fire as James suggests?

"If any of you lack wisdom, let him ask of God, that giveth to all men liberally, and upbraideth not; and it shall be given him." (James 1:5)

PATTERN 2   WISDOM

"The fear of the Lord is the beginning of knowledge: but fools despise wisdom and instruction" (Proverbs 1:7). We are living in an age of great knowledge. There are perhaps more intellectual giants living in our time than ever before. This is an age when men can transplant vital organs, walk on the moon, build massive towers into the heavens, and travel across the ocean in a few short hours.

Today in America there are many unemployed people walking the streets. Many of these unemployed have earned college degrees. The cry of our sophisticated and technological age is not a lack of education, but a lack of wisdom. We are experiencing a poverty of wisdom in contrast to the advance in knowledge. We have the knowledge, but not the spiritual wisdom to use it. This is shown by the alarming increase in crime and corruption, unrest among the minorities, increasing divorce rates, and the general hardening of theological arteries all across the land.

Still, this is the golden age of dishwashers, trash compactors, color television, pocket-size electronic calculators, cassette tape recorders, and the always tempting ubiquitous Master Charge plate.

But what happens when disaster strikes? In the book of Job we find a successful man facing a myriad of disasters. In this period of extreme uncertainty Job asked: "Where shall wisdom be found? and where is the place of understanding? Man knoweth not the price thereof; neither is it found in the land of the living. The depth saith, It is not in me: and the sea saith, It is not with me. It cannot be gotten for gold, neither shall silver be weighed for the price thereof. It cannot be valued with the gold of Ophir, with the precious onyx, or the sapphire. The gold and the crystal cannot equal it: and the exchange of it shall not be for jewels of fine gold. No mention shall be made of coral, or of pearls: for the price of wisdom is above rubies" (Job 28:12-18). He concludes by reiterating: "Whence then cometh wisdom? and where is the place of understanding?" (Job 28:20). The psalmist accepts the challenge of such a question and answers in Psalm 111:10: "The fear of the Lord is the beginning of wisdom."

James writes: "If any of you lack wisdom, let him ask of God, that giveth to all men liberally [or freely], and upbraideth not [doesn't scold for asking]" (1:5). However, James stresses that such an individual must ask in faith without doubting: "For he that wavereth is like a wave of the sea driven with the wind and tossed" (1:6).

If you are like that, one minute this way and the next minute that way, then you are a fickle religious faker. A double-minded man (pardon the expression) is a schizophrenic disciple. This suggests instability in all ways, not just in your church life. When a man is confused in fellowship with the covenant community, he is also confused on Monday morning at the job. He lacks wisdom and sound judgment in all things.

If you lack wisdom, ask it of God. He will give freely. If we had to borrow $10,000 from a bank and were assured we'd get the loan, we might still hesitate because of the consequences. The consequences involve our pledge to pay it all back—with interest!

If all we have to do is ask of God and He freely gives, then why do we hold back? It must be that we're afraid of the consequences. But what are the consequences with God? Does He charge interest like the banker? God doesn't charge an interest rate, but He does ask for a commitment. Some will suggest that the commitment is worse than the banker's interest. We consider it too much for God to ask for total commitment from us. We would prefer a banker rather than God to check our credit rating. The interesting thing is that God already knows our credit rating. In His sight we stand as poor risks.

Then why does God want us to "bank" with Him? You will notice that God is not like any banker on earth. He sent His Son, Jesus, to die for us "while we were yet sinners" (Romans 5:8). At the point when our credit rating stood at zero,

He came to us. You can't find a more gracious banker in the entire universe!

God freely gives wisdom to all who call. In this context then, the wisdom comes through prayer, even as patience comes through tribulation (1:3). The two are closely related. Is there a greater need for wisdom than when we are passing through fiery trials? It is difficult to act wisely when we are suffering. A difficult situation tends to make us tense, impulsive, emotional, and irrational. An easy answer or a shortcut is appealing at such moments. In John Bunyan's *Pilgrim's Progress,* Christian heard lions growling on the other side of a hill. He was tempted to go another way, which seemed easier at the moment. He courageously decided to go on in spite of the growling lions. To his amazement, when he topped the hill he saw the lions chained to a post. He passed them by without harm. He had been tempted to take another route, which would have been much longer and more arduous. The answers to life's difficult problems are not found in shortcuts. A ragged and torn wisdom will suggest shortcuts, but this is not God's way.

In a real sense we are all philosophers. Wisdom itself presents a philosophical problem, for there are two basic schools of thought. There is the Christian approach to wisdom and the non-Christian approach to wisdom. These are two opposite poles of thought. Most people choose the latter approach, which at first appears to be more philosophical and rational. This non-Christian approach eliminates faith and appears as a rational exercise in morality. It tends to tickle the ears upon first hearing. In the end, however, it leaves you dry and empty. It is merely an exercise and definitely not a life-changing one. When we receive wisdom from God it produces a radical change in our lives, a tilt in the opposite direction. The compass of decisions has a different bearing. The needle points to God and not man. This is what happened to Paul on the road to Damascus.

Paul was fighting the contagious news of the resurrection of Jesus. He considered it heresy in light of Judaism proper. The light of Judaism turned out to be darkness, and what he thought darkness turned out to be light! Paul's thinking was radically changed on that day. The new light of wisdom was so overwhelming that it took Paul a long while to update his thinking on the Scriptures.

It is hard to convey this wisdom to the non-Christian world. The philosophy of the world moves at a rapid pace, always changing, but never getting anywhere. It appears to be much like a dog running in circles to chase his tail. The wisdom of the world is subtle, but empty. It is perhaps best described by Albert Camus in the *Myth of Sisyphus.*

Sisyphus is an absurd hero. His whole being is exerted toward accomplishing nothing. He is like a lot of people today. Sisyphus was condemned to pushing a huge stone up a mountain. We find him with his face red, mouth twisted up, cheek tight against the cold stone. His shoulder is bracing the stony mass, foot wedged and muscles bulging, as he strains to move the thing up the mountain. When he reaches the top he sighs in relief, which is only fleeting, because the minute he straightens and releases the stone, down it goes into the valley. Sisyphus treks down to the stone. Again he braces against it, face red, mouth twisted, cheek tight, foot wedged, and up he comes. Upon reaching the summit the same thing happens. In fact, this course of action is repeated over and over. Is there any wisdom in this? Is that what life is all about? There must be more to life than this ever-grinding, fruitless effort.

Jesus said: "My yoke is easy, and my burden is light" (Matthew 11:30). The wisdom of Christ awaits all who would ask for it. You will notice that He doesn't promise clear skies or a nice breeze for smooth sailing thereafter. But He does promise to be our Yokefellow in carrying the burdens! Get His wisdom; it's the best in town.

DISCUSSION-STARTER QUESTIONS

1. Why is the fear of the Lord the beginning of knowledge?

2. Why does God want us to "bank" with Him?

3. Why is it hard to convey the wisdom of Christianity to a non-Christian world?

4. Do Christians ever find themselves acting like Sisyphus?

5. How can Sisyphus escape his ever-grinding, fruitless task?

6. What did Jesus mean by the wise saying: "My yoke is easy and my burden is light"?

7. Does God ever refuse to give His wisdom? Can anyone receive it?

"Let the brother of low degree rejoice in that he is exalted: but the rich, in that he is made low: because as the flower of the grass he shall pass away." (James 1:9, 10)

PATTERN 3   HOW GOD PROMOTES

This passage of Scripture is very important in that it speaks of demotions and promotions. No one wants to be demoted, but everyone wants to be promoted. In God's sight how does this work? Let us keep in mind that James is writing for believers in the covenant community. The world would view demotion and promotion from an entirely different perspective.

"Let the brother of low degree rejoice in that he is exalted" (1:9)—that is promotion. "But the rich, in that he is made low" (1:10)—that is demotion. To understand these two verses we must first attempt to view the world through God's eyes and not ours. In other words, we have to turn our mind's eye inside out, because we look at everything with a finite mind and according to the world's influence. Jesus saw everything from the perspective of the Infinite One. Listen to these words:

"Then said Jesus unto his disciples, If any man

will come after me, let him deny himself, and take up his cross, and follow me. For whosoever will save his life shall lose it: and whosoever will lose his life for my sake shall find it" (Matthew 16:24, 25). He said: "Many that are first shall be last; and the last shall be first" (Matthew 19:30). Also: "The last shall be first, and the first last: for many be called, but few chosen" (Matthew 20:16). Jesus also pointed out: "He that is greatest among you shall be your servant. And whosoever shall exalt himself shall be abased; and he that shall humble himself shall be exalted" (Matthew 23:11, 12).

These statements show that God looks at things from a different perspective. We need to look with the eye of faith to understand how God sees us and the world. The eye of faith helps us to better understand the perspective of God. In this light James writes: "Let the brother of low degree rejoice in that he is exalted" (1:9). James is talking about a saint who has received a promotion, or better position, because of God.

I like the simple rendering of our verse (1:9) as recorded in *The New International Version:* "The brother in humble circumstances ought to take pride in his high position." There are two applications of this promotion. First, there is promotion in the church. The most poverty-stricken man could possibly be the most spiritual-minded man in the congregation. He could be chairman of the deacons or hold some other position of leadership in the fellowship. God has a way of exalting the low things of the world, the base things, and the things despised (1 Corinthians

1:27, 28). So in the church we might find an elevator operator or janitor serving in a very high position, whereas the vice-president of a company might be merely holding down a pew. God's promotion is not based on prestige or position in the world.

The second application deals with the believer in the outside world and not in the covenant community. Keep in mind that the believer, or New Testament word "saint," is one under control of the Holy Spirit. A New Testament saint is Spirit born, Spirit fed, and Spirit led.

I like what a young lady said one night in church, "The believer is under construction by the Holy Spirit." The believer recognizes that he has a long way to go, but the foundation has been laid and the building process has begun!

James tells us that to the world our believing brother will appear to be "of low degree" or perhaps of no account. But to God he is worthy of promotion. Implied in this verse is something extremely important. What the world considers great is not necessarily great in the sight of God. What the world uses as a measuring stick of success is not what God uses.

One of the biggest problems we face is determining the Lord's will. The world's influence makes it difficult to determine what is right. Consider a man named Fred who has been working on his job for five years. It's not the best job in the world, but it's the best job Fred ever held. He gets good pay, generous company benefits, and convenient working hours. It has been easy for him to be a Christian and work at this job. There is no pressure otherwise. Suppose out of the blue another job turns up. Perhaps it's of questionable nature. But, this new job would mean a big promotion, prestige, and a large salary increase. The money is quite tempting and so is the prestigious position.

Satan suggests, "Fred, old boy, why don't you take that job? They really want you, and think of the money you'll be making. You've been saying you needed more money for your daughter's education, so here's your chance. Besides, you can give more to the church!" Satan proceeds to give Fred the red-carpet treatment, "You know, Fred, you're being considered for this job because you're a spiritual man."

"Oh, yea," Fred replies in humility. "Why do you say that?"

Satan continues, "Well, you don't drink, you go to church, and you're a family man. You're the kind of man they want! You're a spiritual man. Fred, this job is from the Lord. He's promoting you!"

It is not impossible for God to be behind a promotion, but you must be quite sure who is doing the promoting—Satan or God. Every time Satan makes an offer to the child of God it always "appears" better than God's offer. Satan's offer appeals to the lust of the flesh, lust of the eye, and to the pride of life (Genesis 3:6). Satan weakens us by deception; one pinch of spirituality and two pinches of carnality. He will suggest we are spiritual, and then appeal to the flesh even by the suggestion.

God never suggests we have "arrived" spiritually, because He knows we have not! Spirituality may be thought of in connection with a process of Christian growth. Growth is maturity—maturing in the Lord.

There are different levels of maturity. A lot depends on when we are born into the kingdom of God, and how we grow after being born. A good formula to remember is: prayer + Bible study = growth (spirituality). Add witnessing to the first half of this formula and it's like adding water and sunshine to a plant. Plants cannot grow without water or sunlight. I question the growth of Christians who never witness or even try to influence someone for Christ. Bible study and prayer will be a catalyst in thrusting us into a witnessing situation.

Satan will always seek to hinder your growth by appealing to the flesh. He will say to you, "You're a better man than this job allows. You don't drink. You're a family man. The other job will pay more money and give you a golden opportunity to witness."

So you pray the prayer of opportunity, "Lord, this is a tough decision. I've been needing more money. I believe You're behind this golden opportunity. I'll take the job! Thanks, Lord. You've been a great help. See You later."

Let's stop kidding ourselves into answering our own prayers. God will answer our prayers—if we give Him the opportunity. The big question is: Should the Christian always avoid worldly promotions? The answer is easy—of course not! Keep in mind that "The Spirit of truth . . . he will guide you into all truth" (John 16:13).

You see, God has a special purpose and calling for each of us. We must prayerfully strive to find that purpose and fulfill that calling. If you really want to know who was behind your promotion, consider the pressures and lack of promises you received. Satan is a liar and will deceive you. Companies may sometimes say, "We're looking for a nondrinking family man," but right away after you get the job, the pressure is on to socialize at cocktail parties.

What can you do if you're already on the job? Should you quit and cast yourself upon the Lord in faith? No, but you can look around and see what the Lord can do through you. Did Daniel quit when he found himself serving the heathen Babylonians? Did Ezekiel quit, or the prophet Jeremiah? No, these men continued to serve God regardless of their predicaments. So can you. Pray that God will use you on your job! God delights in a prayer like that, but watch out, for prayers of such a nature are dangerous. God may take you at your word!

James also writes about demotion when he says the rich ought to rejoice in the fact that they are made low (1:10). To the poor, Jesus said, "Come up." To Zacchaeus He said, "Come down." It is not that God is against wealth. That is not the message of this passage. We often say the root of all evil is money. That's not correct. The love of money is the root of all evil. Jesus said it is difficult for a rich man to enter the kingdom of Heaven because of his material interests (Matthew 19:16-26), but He didn't say it was impossible!

Zacchaeus gave a lot of money away (four-fold), but I'm sure he continued to be better off than the average man. God blesses some with the ability to make money and to be good businessmen. A book in our church library, *God Owns My Business,* verifies this statement. It is by Stanley Tam, and he recognizes his wealth is from God. Mr. Tam turned his business over to God, and God has blessed him.

To the rich young ruler God required similar recognition and stewardship, but the young man turned away sorrowfully. The rich and the poor must humble themselves, and God will promote in His own way and in His own time.

There is one thing we must keep in mind. In order for God to promote He must first demote! We must be brought down before He can take us up. This does not mean that all must crash financially before God can bless. It means that we must crash egotistically, that is, humble ourselves before the Lord.

A ruler of the Jews came to Jesus by night. His name was Nicodemus. He came while it was dark, so that none of his colleagues would know. He inquired as to the kingdom of God. Jesus said: "Except a man be born again" (John 3:3). It was (and still is) so simple. To be born again a man must repent. In order to repent a man must humble himself, whether he be rich or poor. The rich and poor both sin, although the rich may sin in more luxury. The cost, however, is the same—death!

A once-born sinner must come to understand that he is spiritually bankrupt. He has invested in

31

earthly treasures and those mean nothing to God. He must allow God to radically transform him. "For by grace are ye saved through faith; and that not of yourselves: it is the gift of God" (Ephesians 2:8). The born-again man now has an investment in the kingdom of Heaven, and God gives unlimited bank accounts! The redeemed sinner is now available for God's promotion.

DISCUSSION-STARTER QUESTIONS

1. What is the world's view of demotion and promotion? Has the covenant community (church) been influenced by this viewpoint?

2. What is spirituality?

3. Do you agree that every time Satan makes an offer to the child of God it always appears better than God's offer?

4. Have you ever prayed the prayer of opportunity?

5. Should the Christian always view wordly promotion as evil? Did Daniel accept wordly promotion? Who really promoted Daniel?

6. Do you agree that for God to promote He must first demote?

7. In what way are we all demoted before we can be promoted?

8. What is meant by the statement that God gives unlimited bank accounts? Do we really believe that? Do we use it?

> "Blessed is the man that endureth temptation: for when he is tried, he shall receive the crown of life, which the Lord hath promised to them that love him. Let no man say when he is tempted, I am tempted of God: for God cannot be tempted with evil, neither tempteth he any man."
> (James 1:12, 13)

PATTERN 4   TEMPTATION

"Every good gift and every perfect gift is from above, and cometh down from the Father of lights, with whom is no variableness, neither shadow of turning" (1:17).

Our God is immutable. Once He has set the earth spinning on its axis, it spins on its axis. Once He has decreed that the sun shall give light and heat to our solar system, it gives light and heat. Once He has declared: "Without shedding of blood is no remission [for sin]" (Hebrews 9:22), then only through the shed blood is remission found. He has given His Son to fulfill that! Once He has declared: "Every good gift and every perfect gift is from above," we can rest assured that only goodness comes from His hands.

There is an erroneous rustle in the treetops that God tempts us. This immutable and perfect God never does that! We must dispel that rumor now. God does not tempt or make solicitation to sin. It is against His nature to tempt man.

James says: "Let no man say when he is tempted, I am tempted of God: for God cannot be tempted with evil, neither tempteth He any man" (1:13). God does not solicit us to do evil, nor do we have the ability to tempt God. What do we have within our means to tempt the Creator? Can the tiny minnow tempt the mammoth whale? Can the lowly ant tempt the majestic elephant? The creature has nothing within his grasp to tempt the Creator. The grace of it all is that the Creator never tempts the creatures whom He has made. Then how, under the canopy of grace, is man tempted? What is held before man that entices him to sin?

The popular saying for sin or any wrongdoing is "The devil made me do it." There is probably more truth there than people realize. What makes a man sin? Why throw away life, family, and reputation for a season of sin? If a person would just weigh the consequences or use some rationality, perhaps he would see the dire and inevitable results of sin.

David was one of Israel's greatest kings. He expanded the borders of the tiny nation and brought her to the zenith of power. He nearly lost all in one fleeting season of premeditated sin. David repented, but the sword of division never left his house.

Sin seems to be like a gift wrapped with the prettiest ribbon, the most colorful paper, and in the most interesting shape of box. The problem is that we can't wait to look inside that box. There is a mysterious attraction about it that gnaws at our brain. We can't stand it. Any box that beautiful must contain some marvelous gift. We shake it with care, for fear we might break the contents. We hold it to the light, in hopes of seeing without opening. We sit and think: What would fit in a box that size? Finally, in a fit of uncontrollable and willful indulgence we tear into the box. Our imagination has been so whetted, that usually we are disappointed. What we find is vastly different from what we expected.

Temptation is always like that. The appeal isn't really the color of ribbon, or beauty of the wrapping paper, or even the size of the box. We can stand that. But it's the ubiquitous writhing worm of mystery that lies on top our brain and whispers ever so softly, "Hey, you don't know what I am."

You cannot hide sin. It's impossible. Sin is like serpents sunning on the rocks. They crawl out of their hiding places to lie exposed to the sun. When a man is involved in sin he has opened Pandora's box, and it's sure self-destruction.

The question once again is: Why succumb to the tempter's snare? Here is James's answer: "Every man is tempted, when he is drawn away of his own lust, and enticed" (1:14). Here is the explanation. Each person is drawn away by his own lusts (internal) and enticed (external). Temptation is a smooth, two-headed coin. In the Garden of Eden there was first the suggestion of the serpent that eating the forbidden fruit would make Eve wise and like a god. This was enticement, and external. The enticement was consummated by the appeal to Eve's inner lust for the fruit. The inner lust was representative of the internal part of temptation.

The enticement itself is not defiling. Only when the external, or enticement, is consummated with the internal lusts, is sin born. If there is no appeal to desire, there is no temptation. The habitual thief is not tempted to steal if placed on a barren island by himself. Not all persons have the same evil desires. An evil desirable to one is perhaps repulsive to another. The archtempter is a skilled craftsman in knowing what appeals to each person.

Since the original fall, man's inclination is to sin. Fallen man loves darkness more than he loves light (John 3:19). Presently, fallen Genesis man is living in an abnormal state; he is not living in his natural, created way. The inclination of original Genesis man was to serve God. He knew nothing of sin. As sinners we are abnormal before God. Abnormal man is not Genesis man in the garden, but the wild scoundrel outside the garden. Jesus came to make abnormal man normal again!

It is only in Christ that our spiritual pulse beats normally. In Christ we experience the tranquillity of Eden and we can overcome our temptations to break from this scene.

DISCUSSION-STARTER QUESTIONS

1. Describe the difference between a temptation and a test. Why is it necessary for God to test us?

2. Do you think we are ever tempted beyond what we can endure? (1 Corinthians 10:13)

3. Do you agree that temptation usually is disguised in gift wrapping?

4. What do you think about the popular saying, "The devil made me do it"?

5. What does fallen Genesis man consider as an abnormal person? Would God agree with fallen man's view of normal and abnormal?

6. Should we feel guilty about being tempted? When does temptation become sin?

7. Can normal man (born-again) rise above temptation?

"Every good gift and every perfect gift is from above, and cometh down from the Father of lights, with whom is no variableness, neither shadow of turning. Of his own will begat he us with the word of truth, that we should be a kind of first-fruits of his creatures." (James 1:17, 18)

PATTERN 5   BORN FREE

In the very beginning God made everything just right. Everything God made was absolutely perfect, without blemish. This included Adam and Eve. Every gift that He gave to them was good and perfect. Utopia, which man dreams of, had been created by God. Adam and Eve experienced the joys of utopian living. Complete harmony and bliss existed in the garden until the catastrophic fall. Afterward, all the king's horses and all the king's men couldn't put Eden back together again. The perfection of Eden had vanished. Now Adam and Eve were different. They had to live with the haunting memories of what they once had possessed, but then lost. Adam and Eve were driven from the garden and forced to work and struggle for their existence.

Physical birth took place with the arrival of Cain, and then Abel. Later, when Adam was one hundred thirty years old, Seth was born (Genesis 5:3). The process of multiplying and replenishing the earth had begun. God, however, wasn't finished with man. He sought to redeem him from his fallen state. A promise began to reverberate from the lips of the prophets that a Redeemer would come. This One would be born of woman and be a Deliverer.

He would show man how to live and how to die. His death would bring life to all who believe. He would be called Jesus and would be living proof that God is the Creator of Heaven and earth. God would humble himself and identify with man (Philippians 2:5-8). The Spirit of the living God would take on the blue jeans of flesh!

The bloodstream of humanity was invaded by God of His own free will. Jesus taught that in order to be born free, a man must be born again. Nicodemus queried one night: "How can a man be born when he is old?" (John 3:4). Jesus told him that the second birth is not of the flesh, but of the Spirit. We are saved by grace through faith (Ephesians 2:8). For the first time in his religious life, Nicodemus was faced with radical thinking. It wasn't traditional to contemplate a spiritual birth. Previously, God had led man by a pillar of cloud during the day and a pillar of fire at night. Now the revelation was that God desires to dwell within man!

James shares this radical thinking. He claims God has given us many good and perfect things, but the most precious gift is salvation. God doesn't always give us what we want, but He gives us what we need. What we need most is salvation, and he has provided a means for that.

Plato, one of the world's greatest thinkers,

conceived of the ideal state. He described this utopian state in *The Republic.* Our forefathers sought to establish an ideal state, which would afford man freedom to fulfill his innermost dreams. They came close in the Declaration of Independence, but this document hasn't provided a utopian state. God gave Moses the Ten Commandents for the Israelite children. The Decalogue was the most perfect document ever received by man because it came straight from God. Yet utopia did not develop in the wilderness, nor later in the land of promise. the problem, then, lies with imperfect man.

Children sometimes play a game in which the one who is "it" is supposed to have a corroded touch. The one with the corroded touch must chase and touch others to corrode them. Man is like that. He often corrodes what he touches. Sometimes even the most perfect gifts are marred in the hands of imperfect man.

James states that God is capable of giving only good and perfect gifts. We are responsible stewards of these gifts. We are to practice stewardship even with the precious gift of salvation. We are truly His special creation for the performance of good works. Paul writes: "For we are his workmanship, created in Christ Jesus unto good works" (Ephesians 2:10). Teenagers sing about getting excited and telling everybody that Jesus Christ is King! Is there a better way of being a steward of salvation? I doubt it.

There is joy in thinking, "Of his own will begat he us" (1:18). Our salvation is entirely free. No one ever paid God an insurance premium to cover a spiritual birth. Jesus' blood paid the entire bill.

We are begotten by the will of God with the Word of truth. The Word of God is powerful and sharp, like a two-edged sword, dividing the soul and spirit (Hebrews 4:12). But it is also like an acupuncture needle. When the Word slips into the mind of man, making the tiniest needle-like hole, pressure is released. The sin tumor has been penetrated! Man is born again! God penetrates us with the slender needle of truth. Isn't it amazing what His Word can do?

Henry Ward Beecher was once asked who had the most influence on his life. He immediately replied, "My father's black servant!" As a boy, Beecher used to lie in bed listening to his father's servant reading from the Word of God. Beecher said, "That poor servant would laugh and cry and shout for joy as he read God's Word." The privilege of hearing God's Word read with such involvement influenced Beecher's life.

Until we have experienced rebirth, the Word pricks our conscience and makes us very uncomfortable. "For all have sinned, and come short of the glory of God" (Romans 3:23). We are, without Christ, like a race horse pulling up lame or a runner with a muscle spasm. Spiritual muscle spasms can be treated only by His Word.

I remember in one of my philosophy classes we debated about absolute truths. The absolute truth for mankind is that Jesus died to make men free. The world holds to bits and pieces of truth, but not to this absolute truth. James calls us to the absolute truth. It's like a canopy of grace over the head of man. This canopy of grace will burst only when we look up in faith. Faith punctures the canopy and brings refreshing showers of blessings.

But what is truth? Pilate once asked Jesus this very question (John 18:38). How could Pilate have missed the truth when it was right before his eyes? Perhaps Pilate's concept of God got in the way. He was expecting God to come down like a mighty rocket, scorching the earth and roaring like thunder. A perspiring Jesus with a bleeding back and thorn-pressed brow didn't meet this concept. To Pilate, Jesus was too much flesh and blood to be God!

Only God could have conceived such a plan. No man took part in the planning of redemption. It came straight from the portals of Heaven—a free plan of redemption.

Years ago, in the Northwest, there was an Indian chief who had been converted to Christianity. Before his conversion the chief had been known by the settlers as "the meanest Indian west of the Rockies."

Another chief came up to him one day and said, "Why is it you're always talking about Jesus? What has this Man done for you?"

The converted Indian took a number of chips of wood and made a circle on the ground. He dug for a worm, put it in the middle of the circle, and then set the circle on fire. As the fire spread round the worm, it sought for safety, but could not find it. When the flames were at their hottest, the chief burned his own hand as he thrust it into the circle of flames and lifted the worm out of danger. Putting it in a place of safety, he turned to his fellow chief and said, "I am that worm. Here in this world I have been wounded by sin and temptation. I almost died because of my evil deeds. God came in the form of Jesus Christ and freely took me, worm that I was, out of the flame of sin. He rescued me. My salvation is a free gift of His own will."

Let us not forget, God came and freely put on the blue jeans of flesh. This means He actually laid aside His princely garments of divinity, so that He might identify with man. And He did all of this of His own free will.

DISCUSSION-STARTER QUESTIONS

1. What does salvation cost us?

2. What is the best way to be a steward of salvation?

3. Does God ever give us something that is contrary to our wish? If so, why?

4. If salvation is a free gift, how does faith enter the picture?

5. What are some misconceptions about God that people have today?

PATTERN 6   ANGER

Someone has said, "A man in a passion rides a wild horse." Another wise sage suggests, "Speak when you're angry and you'll make the best speech you'll ever regret." James writes in typical blue jeans fashion: "Let every man be swift to hear, slow to speak, and slow to wrath" (1:19).

Edgar Allen Poe wrote a wonderful short story entitled "Black Cat." In this story the husband describes his wife's black cat as the perfect personification of evil. One day as the husband is going into the basement, the cat trips him. The man becomes so angry that he is about to kill the cat. The wife comes to the rescue of the cat, and in a fit of anger the man kills his wife. In the basement is a false fireplace. He places the body of his wife in the fireplace and bricks it up, covering his crime. After the neighbors become suspicious, the police are called to the house. They search for the missing woman. They go from the attic down to the basement. The husband leads the way, confident his crime cannot be discovered. When he reaches the basement, he taps his cane on the fireplace saying, "This is a sturdy house, isn't it, officer?" Suddenly a wailing sound comes out of the fireplace. The police proceed to dismantle the fireplace, and to their amazement they find the corpse of the missing woman. Her black cat is alive and sitting on top of her body!

Anger always has a way of coming back on you. The old man in Poe's story had lost everything in one uncontrollable fit of anger. How much better to give a soft answer than to fly off the handle. We need to learn that "A soft answer turneth away wrath: but grievous words stir up anger" (Proverbs 15:1).

James sees true Christians as "doers of the word, and not hearers only" (1:22). A Christian exercises spiritually by putting into practice the truths he hears. His time spent in the pew is not merely to catch up on his rest!

Every sincere believer understands he is in the world, but not of the world. Neil Armstrong became the first human to set foot on the moon. All of America was glued to the television set watching Armstrong's historical feat. Armstrong kept in constant touch with Houston Control on earth. Everything was well planned and controlled, even though he was within the gravitational pull of another celestial body. He was in space, but not of space. Communication with earth was essential for his safety. The Christian must maintain open communications with the Holy Spirit if he is to survive spiritually. His life is one under control of the Holy Spirit. Anger can be overcome only by help from the Holy Spirit.

Paul says: "Let your speech be alway with grace, seasoned with salt" (Colossians 4:6). That smacks of spiritual control. No man can have a seasoned tongue without the Spirit's control.

We have an Adamic nature. But thanks be to God we are made in His image. Because of this we have an inclination of will, which shows up on our spiritual tachometer. In man there is the positive and the negative. The positive is doing His will, whereas the negative is self-will. Self-will is the Adamic nature to love darkness more than light. Our spiritual tachometer does not register when we exhibit self-will. A regenerated man seeks to do God's will, which is positive. The more we submit to His will the farther the tach needle points to service and godliness. He takes over and our lives become positive for Him. The more we neglect spiritual things, the more negative we become. This causes self-will to become more evident, which leads us in direct opposition to God. Self-will thus becomes the red area (negative side) and man's danger zone. It is in this area that man literally blows his stack. He cannot cope with frustration, tension, disappointment, etc. Self-will is often devastating. Anything other than God's will short-circuits a spiritual system. Any angry outburst short-circuits the system. Paul wrote: "Be ye angry, and sin not" (Ephesians 4:26). Paul saw a great danger in allowing anger to fester into a boil!

Seneca said, "The greatest remedy for anger is

delay." I would like to suggest that the greatest remedy is to delay *and* pray. Prayer will cause you to think before you bareback ride the wild horse of anger! Prayer will cause you to saddle the horse, and with bit and bridle you will ride off in complete control.

Abe Lincoln used to write letters which he later threw away. I imagine we have all written a steaming hot letter that we decided, in a cooler moment, not to send. A moment of steaming anger can destroy and be costly.

A scientist had a servant who exasperated him by his stupidity. One day, when the servant was more stupid than usual, the angry scientist threw a book at his head. The servant ducked, and the book flew out of the window.

"Now, go and pick up that book!" ordered the scientist. The servant started to obey, but a passerby had walked off with the book. The scientist thereupon began to wonder what book he had thrown away. To his horror, he discovered that it was a quaint and rare volume on mathematics, which he had purchased for fifty dollars in London.

"The next time I feel it is absolutely necessary to throw things," he exclaimed, "I'll choose something less expensive than a favorite book!"

But his troubles were not over. The weeks went by, and time had begun to assuage his grief. One day after strolling into a secondhand bookstore, he perceived to his great delight a copy of the book he had lost. He asked the price.

"Well," said the dealer reflectively, "I guess we can let you have it for forty dollars. It's a pretty rare book, and I daresay I could get seventy-five dollars by holding on to it awhile."

The man of science pulled out his wallet and produced the money, delighted at the opportunity of replacing his lost treasure. When he reached home, he sat down to gloat over his find. A card dropped out of the book. The card was his own, and further examination showed that he had bought back his own property. Forty dollars' worth of temper!

Anger is the cause of more man-hours lost, more homes broken, more jobs lost, more people hurt, and more souls lost than perhaps any other sin.

In a fit of anger, Alexander the Great killed his beloved friend and general, Clitus. All future military stratagems of Alexander were affected by that one enraged thrust of the spear. The spreading of the Hellenic influence was dealt an unkind blow by anger.

"The wrath of man worketh not the righteousness of God," according to James (1:20). Moses killed the Egyptian, smote the rock, and broke the tablets of stone. We might excuse Moses by saying it was righteous wrath. Remember, however, Moses never entered the promise land! Was it anger that kept him out?

Anger is like a sudden whirlwind. It is vinegar to the teeth and smoke to the eyes. James urges us: "Lay apart all filthiness and superfluity of naughtiness" (1:21). Doesn't this describe an angry outburst, a volcanic eruption?

I believe God speaks to us through His Word, and He can help us control anger. The book of

Proverbs is a book of spiritual prescriptions. It shows us how to get along with fellowman. If an apple a day will help keep the doctor away, one chapter of Proverbs a day will help keep the devil away. Try it and see. Life becomes less complicated if we trust God and apply the words of James: "Let every man be swift to hear, slow to speak, slow to wrath."

DISCUSSION-STARTER QUESTIONS

1. Is self-will the same thing as free will?

2. Is there a difference between anger and righteous wrath?

3. Is the Christian never to lose his temper?

4. Is Lincoln's letter-writing policy a good remedy for overcoming anger?

5. What would be the difference in counting to ten, or quoting Proverbs (or James) when you're angry?

6. Do you think reading the Bible helps keep the devil away?

7. How can the Holy Spirit help combat anger?

"If ye fulfil the royal law according to the scripture, Thou shalt love thy neighbour as thyself, ye do well: but if ye have respect to persons, ye commit sin, and are convinced of the law as transgressors." (James 2:8, 9)

PATTERN 7 BROTHERLY LOVE

James maintains, with his blue jeans theology, that Christianity is the best. Best not only because of doctrine, but because it works in life. No other religion can do so much for man. No other religion offers the comforting presence of the Holy Spirit.

In pattern 1 we saw the application in the midst of trials. Christ is a present help in trials. James isn't dodging anything. He is saying there will be difficult times, but Christ is with us. After every storm the sun shines through. Now James has set the stage by showing that nothing good and lasting is easy. We have always known that, but we tend to forget. We know many things that we refuse to recognize in our minds. There is much back there, in our heads, clamoring to be heard. As chairman we gravel our thoughts down and say, "You are out of order; I don't care to hear from you now." We go on our obstinate way flaunting our will against His will. That's why we have so much difficulty.

We have now reached a point in our study where we must see faith tested by brotherly love. Perhaps this is the most severe test. It's sometimes very difficult to love the unlovely or ones who would take advantage of you. James is referring to the need to love your brother as yourself (2:8), regardless of the brother! James probably remembered our Lord's story of the good Samaritan as he wrote: "If ye fulfil the royal law according to the scripture, Thou shalt love thy neighbour as thyself, ye do well" (2:8).

We are told: "Have not the faith of our Lord Jesus Christ, the Lord of glory, with respect of persons" (2:1). It doesn't matter to the Lord whether you're rich, poor, famous, unknown, or what color your skin is, or where you live, or what you accomplish materially on earth. He's concerned with the choices you make. These choices dictate your destiny.

James has touched upon a very sensitive point. He has seen a common sin that is still prevalent today, the sin of being a respecter of persons. You and I both know what he means. The needs of our church programs cause us to show partiality and favoritism to the rich and famous.

For instance, when a doctor moves into town, often the churches fall over one another trying to woo him into their congregation. Or suppose Hal Lindsey moved to town. Think of the prestige and drawing power to have Mr. Lindsey as a member of your church. You could write your friends across the state line and say, "Today I sat in the same pew with the late great planet earth!"

A letter would come back from your friend saying, "So you sat with the late great planet earth. That's nothing. A month ago I was right beside the cross and the switchblade!"

But let's keep this in proper perspective. I believe we should give credit to whom credit is due. The Christian knows that all credit is due God. Without Him we are nothing. In God's work each man is shaped for the hour. God does the shaping and God chooses the hour!

James isn't condemning the wealthy or famous. Neither is he despising the poor. He is condemning the church program that is shaped and molded to catch certain people.

Listen to my version of this passage: "My brethren, you claim the Lord Jesus Christ as your own, and show favoritism. If a man comes into your church with gold on his fingers, dressed in a fine polyester suit, and another comes in with worn blue jeans, and you quickly go up to the well-dressed man and point out a comfortably padded pew; whereas you say in passing to the man in worn blue jeans, 'You may stand back there or sit on the floor,' then you have become partial. And isn't this sin?"

But James hits the mark with the inference that partiality and favoritism exist. Today the interest is: "Where do you work? How much education do you have? and Where do you live?" The same sin is as prevalent today as it was in the early church.

Can you see what James has done? He has jammed us smack into the world's standard of values. The Christian has a different set of values. His perspective is from God to earth, not earth to God. God comes first.

The world chooses heroes according to fame and fortune. Have you hit 715 home runs? Have you walked on the moon? Have you written a best-seller? Have you had a smash recording or starred in a television series? These things make the world bug-eyed. I grant that I'm impressed with such things as Hank Aaron's accomplishment and Neil Armstrong's historical feat. But the world isn't giving any accolades to the Man of Calvary. The world's values stack up differently compared with God's. Unfortunately we Christians are often so bombarded that our values become a compromised version of secular society.

Vance Havner has said, "Here gold sells for over forty-five dollars an ounce. In Heaven they pave the streets with it!" Here the last starts at the end of the line and the first at the beginning. There, the last are first and the first last. Here promotion is the thing. There demotion comes first. Here we ask, "What do I get out of it?" There we say, "How can I give more?"

Remember the story Jesus told in Luke 16? Here's how I see it. A certain rich man lived in luxury. One day a beggar by the name of Lazarus came to his door. All the beggar wanted was leftovers. Finally, the beggar died (he probably starved to death) and was taken to the abode of the righteous dead. The rich man also died (probably a coronary from starchy foods), and his soul went to Hell. In Hell his time came to use the telescopic lens fixed on the edge of Hell. He inserted a dime, his last remaining earthly possession, and focused the lens on Paradise far off. There he saw Lazarus in the luxury of the righteous. Everything had changed. Now Lazarus had abundance, and the rich man of earth had nothing, not even a drop of water!

In his abundance the rich man neglected to show love to a brother in need. The tables had turned after death. James urges us to love our neighbor. By doing so we fulfill the law of Christ.

Years ago in a little frontier town nestled against the Sierra mountains, there lived two brothers. They decided to part and strike out in different directions to make a name for themselves. If one became wealthy then he would call the other and help him. One brother went to San Francisco where he became a shoe salesman.

He was so successful he purchased his own store. In a few years he bought another store and then another. Ten years passed, and by then he was quite wealthy. He forgot about his brother.

One day a beggar stumbled into a shoe store. The beggar was barefooted and his torn clothes reeked of alcohol. The beggar asked if they had any old shoes they might give him. The clerks were disturbed, so they went to the owner. He ordered them to throw the man out of the store. He was bad for business, for customers were leaving in disgust. The clerks shoved the beggar out into the dusty street, and he stumbled into the path of a team of horses. The horses panicked and trampled the beggar to death.

A crowd gathered. The wealthy brother came out of the store and walked to the dead man. "It's not your fault," he said consoling his distraught salesmen. "He's just a drunk."

"Who was he?" someone asked.

The brother reached into the beggar's pocket and pulled out a crumpled picture. "Looks like he's been carrying this for some time." He looked at the picture. "Why, that's incredible. This is a picture of my mother!" He turned the body over and looked into the face of the beggar. To his horror he discovered it was his brother!

"If ye fulfil the royal law according to the scripture, Thou shalt love thy neighbour as thyself, ye do well: but if ye have respect to persons, ye commit sin, and are convinced of the law as transgressors" (2:8, 9).

DISCUSSION-STARTER QUESTIONS

1. What is the difference between Christianity and religion?

2. Do you believe our choices dictate our destiny?

3. Do you agree that James condemns the church program designed to catch certain people?

4. How can the Christian know that his values are according to God's approval?

5. Do you feel the church has compromised its values?

6. Do you see any comparison between the rich man and Lazarus (Luke 16), and the wealthy shoe salesman?

"What doth it profit, my
brethren, though a man say
he hath faith, and have not
works? can faith save
him?" (James 2:14)
"Even so faith, if it hath not
works, is dead, being
alone." (James 2:17)

PATTERN 8   BLUE JEANS FAITH

The great reformer, Martin Luther, had some
problems with this letter. He called it a "right
strawy epistle," because he couldn't reconcile
James's position of works with Paul's position of
faith. Paul said: "By grace are ye saved through
faith; and that not of yourselves: it is the gift of
God: not of works, lest any man should boast"
(Ephesians 2:8, 9).

James makes contrasting statements: "What
doth it profit, my brethren, though a man say he
hath faith, and have not works? can faith save
him?" (2:14) and "Faith, if it hath not works, is
dead, being alone" (2:17). James proposes that
works is a direct result of faith. He doesn't contradict Paul. The Holy Spirit isn't striving against
himself! James simply emphasizes a saving faith.
And saving faith is a working faith. Paul would
agree when he said: "Work out your own salvation with fear and trembling" (Philippians 2:12).

Martin Luther wasn't, or isn't, the only one to

have trouble with faith and works. We have problems reconciling the two thoughts today. We have talked so much about grace that we've become grace-bound. Now this isn't to pigeon-hole grace in any way. He has saved us of His own will. James recognizes the problem of grace-bound Christians. They have come to rest on grace, and then do nothing else.

Jesus summed up all the commandments by urging us to love God with all we have, and then to love our neighbor as ourself. That is putting your grace muscles to the task of influencing people for Christ, and that involves works. It calls for a blue jeans faith, a working faith. We are His masterpieces unto good works! Jesus Christ is the artist of our lives.

Did you ever have a spiritual diagnostic check? Well, Dr. James gives one free! Look at James 2:14-26. If someone is in need of food and clothing, and you say, "I'll start the deacon prayer chain rolling," and you leave that needy person, what have you done? James believes the Christian shows his faith by his good works. He puts his billfold and his time on the line for a needy brother. This entire letter is a course in applied Christianity.

Remember the story of the good Samaritan? A man fell among thieves and was beaten and robbed. He was left in a semiconscious state along the roadside. A priest passed by on the other side, and then a Levite did the same thing. Finally a Samaritan came down the road. He saw the wounded man and had compassion. He went to him in spite of the fact that it might have been a trick. The Samaritan dressed his wounds and took him to the nearest inn. There he remained overnight with him, paid the bill, and said, "Take care of him; and whatsoever thou spendest more, when I come again, I will repay thee" (Luke 10:35). That is blue jeans faith in action. That is precisely what James is talking about.

In John Bunyan's classic, *Pilgrim's Progress,* Christian met Talkative on his journey to the Heavenly City. The problem with Talkative was his religion. It was on his tongue! He talked a good game, but he did nothing to show it. What is the old worn cliche? "I can't hear what you're saying because of what you are!"

Sometimes I think we're indolent as Christians. I am as guilty as you are. We enjoy the comforts of the air-conditioned building and padded pew, but we rarely venture into the heat of the market-place. Perhaps we have become like the North African church of Augustine's day. Great theologians debated doctrines and talked of missions, but they did nothing. This missionless church crumbled before Mohammed and his followers!

We are like the California farmer who was sitting, doing nothing, under a shade tree in the middle of the afternoon. A busy neighbor happened by.

"What are you doing sitting there?" he asked.

"Just sitting and waiting," the farmer replied.

"Waiting? Waiting for what?" the neighbor queried.

"It's like this," said the farmer. "Two days ago I cut some brush. Lightning struck the brush pile and burned it up for me. Then yesterday I decided to cut down a huge oak tree, but a strong wind did it for me. Now I'm sitting here waiting for an earthquake to shake the potatoes out of the ground!"

We sit in the shade of the pew waiting for God to shake the sinners to life for us. Blue jeans faith is faith in action. Mental assent is not enough.

A man bought passage on a stagecoach. He noticed that the tickets all cost the same, but some were given different classifications. There were first class, second class, and third class tickets. Along the way they came to a steep incline. The driver stopped the stagecoach and said, "All first class passengers sit tight. Second class passengers get out and walk. Third class, get out and push!" In our churches we have first class, second class, and third class pew riders. We need more third class pushers. If James were here today, he probably would suggest more blue-collar workers of faith.

The perfect example of this blue jeans faith is found in the illustration of Abraham and Rahab. When was Abraham counted righteous? He was counted righteous long before his trip to Mount Moriah with his son Isaac. Abraham had faith in God. But his faith was tested and put to work in going to Mount Moriah. There upon Mount Moriah he stood justified before God because of his willingness to place his beloved son Isaac on the altar of sacrifice. The willingness to sacrifice what we love the most shows where our heart lies. Abraham's faith was made perfect by his works.

Likewise Rahab, the harlot, stood justified by her works. But when did faith enter her heart? She said to the Israelite spies: "I know that the Lord hath given you the land, and that your terror is fallen upon us, and that all the inhabitants of the land faint because of you. For we have heard how the Lord dried up the water of the Red sea for you, when ye came out of Egypt; and what ye did unto the two kings of the Amorites, that were on the other side of the Jordan, Sihon and Og, whom ye utterly destroyed. And as soon as we had heard these things, our hearts did melt . . ." (Joshua 2:9-11). Rahab believed in the might of the Lord before she saw the spies in the land. Her faith was justified by her works of hiding the spies and helping them escape.

Perhaps the whole thing can be summed up by repeating what James said: "Even so faith, if it hath not works, is dead, being alone" (2:17).

A wealthy man was led to the Lord. He became a zealous worker in the church, calling on people and teaching a Sunday-school class. One day another Christian asked, "Why is it you give so much time to the Lord? You are a busy man. All you need to do is give your money."

The wealthy man replied, "God has placed us in His vineyard. We weren't placed here to eat the grapes, but to hoe them!"

What God needs is more people willing to hoe and to work—more people with a blue jeans faith.

DISCUSSION-STARTER QUESTIONS

1. Why do you think Martin Luther was unable to reconcile the position of James with that of Paul?

2. What does Paul mean by "work out your own salvation with fear and trembling" (Philippians 2:12)?

3. What do we mean by grace-bound?

4. Do you think Rahab was a saved person? If so, when was she saved?

5. Why was Abraham asked to offer Isaac?

"But the tongue can no man tame; it is an unruly evil, full of deadly poison." (James 3:8)

PATTERN 9 A MOVING SUBJECT

"It was a very little word, only the other day.
It was a very naughty word, I had not meant to say.
But it was not really lost, when from my lips it flew.
My little brother picked it up, and now he says it too."

I can't remember where I learned that little poem, but it directs our attention to a very moving subject—the tongue. Tongue control is one of the crying needs of the church today. Schisms, divisiveness, and other severe dislocations of the body are caused by the tongue.

"But the tongue can no man tame; it is an unruly evil, full of deadly poison. Therewith bless we God, even the Father; and therewith curse we men, which are made after the similitude of God. Out of the same mouth proceedeth blessing and cursing. My brethren, these things ought not so to be" (James 3:8-10).

In his play, *Much Ado About Nothing*, Shakespeare wrote, "He hath a heart as sound as a bell, and his tongue is the clapper; for what his heart thinks his tongue speaks" (Act III, scene 2).

That which goes on inside a man eventually spills out on the tip of his tongue. James sees the tongue as a mirror to the heart. Socrates must have seen the same thing when he wrote, "Speak, friend, that I may see thee."

James attacks the problem by telling it like it is. There were many who wanted to teach, but few willing to be taught. Everyone had his two bits to add, but no one had much of anything to say! "My brethren, be not many masters, knowing that we shall receive the greater condemnation" (3:1). The problem was arrogance and pride. Perhaps some were even boasting of their salvation. Others relished describing their sinful behavior before conversion, as if they were proud of it. Some prided themselves on how much they knew. Everyone was critical of those sincere believers who tried to teach in Christ. It was a dismal situation.

James said: "In many things we offend all. If any man offend not in word, the same is a perfect man, and able also to bridle the whole body" (3:2). None of us are perfect. One evidence of this is the uncontrollable nature of the tongue. Just when we think we have it under control, it strikes again, like a serpent from under a bush!

Man has been given dominion over all things. He can control tigers, lions, elephants, and even whales. He puts a bit in the mouth of a horse to control its direction. He builds huge ocean-going vessels and controls them with a little rudder. He can control a rocket and ride it to the moon and back. But he cannot control the tongue. "Even so the tongue is a little member, and boasteth great things. Behold, how great a matter a little fire kindleth!" (3:5).

One of the smallest members of the body, the tongue, causes the greatest damage. A little boy made an unkind remark, which he later regretted. He told his father about the incident, and that he desired to take back what had been said.

His father gave him a tube of toothpaste and said, "Squeeze all the toothpaste out onto the table." The little boy did it.

"Now put the toothpaste back without breaking open the tube. I'll return in an hour," ordered the father.

The boy worked trying to get the toothpaste back into the tube. He used a spoon, a knife, his mother's nail file, his fingers, his mouth, and anything and everything! He had toothpaste on his hands, elbows, face, and even in his hair. But, he couldn't get it back into the tube. The father returned.

"Father, this is impossible. I can't get the toothpaste back into the tube," said the boy.

"That's right," said the father. "You can't put the toothpaste back, and you can't take back the unkind remarks you've said. You cannot undo what's been done. You must ask forgiveness and pray that no further harm is done."

Just as one little spark or flip of a cigarette may start a roaring forest fire, one little remark may destroy a reputation. "The tongue is a fire, a world of iniquity: so is the tongue among our members, that it defileth the whole body, and setteth on fire the course of nature; and it is set on fire of hell" (3:6). There is so much inconsistency in man. Man controls birds, beasts, and serpents, but not the tongue. The tongue remains "an unruly evil, full of deadly poison" (3:8).

One woman made a slanderous remark about her neighbor. She went to her priest in remorse and confessed her sin. She wished to make atonement. The priest suggested, "Go to the marketplace today and purchase a chicken. Pluck the chicken and drop the feathers at every house along the way until you reach home, then come to see me early tomorrow."

The woman obeyed and dropped feathers all along the way. The next day she arose early and returned to the priest. "I have done what you told me to do," she said.

"Now go pick up all the feathers you dropped and bring them to me," ordered the priest.

The woman searched all over town, but could find only three feathers. With a weary heart she returned to the priest. "Father, I did what you said. But today I could find only three feathers!"

"Exactly," said the priest. "Just as the feathers have blown all over town so have your words gone from house to house. You cannot reclaim them. The harm is done. Beg forgiveness of the Lord and see that you do not sin like this again!"

"Behold, how great a matter a little fire kindleth!" (3:5). In 1871 a cow kicked over a single lantern in the Chicago area. That little flame became a roaring fire that finally devoured 17,450 buildings in an area of about three square miles.

One lantern caused millions of dollars of damage. How much damage can one little tongue do? "Therewith bless we God, even the Father; and therewith curse we men, which are made after the similitude of God" (3:9).

In one of La Fontaine's fables, a servant by the name of Aesop was asked to prepare a banquet. The master ordered Aesop to find the best meat available for the banquet. Aesop went out and bought many tongues. After cooking them, he put them on the table and covered each one with a lid. When the guests were seated, the master ordered the banquet to begin. Each guest removed the lid and found a cooked tongue. The master was furious. He called Aesop aside and said, "You fool, I ordered you to get the best and you went out and bought tongues."

"But master, I got the best," Aesop replied. "Tongues have been responsible for some of the world's greatest sayings and most profound truths. That's why I bought tongues."

"Very well, Aesop, we're going to have another banquet," said the master. "Only this time I want you to buy the worst meat you can find!" Aesop thought awhile, and then went out and bought more tongues.

He cooked them and again placed on the table each tongue, covered with a lid. the guests arrived and were seated. The banquet began. When the master saw what had happened he was absolutely enraged. He ordered Aesop to make explanation at once. Aesop said. "Master, hear me out. You first wanted the best and I bought tongues, because tongues have uttered some of the world's greatest truths. Then you ordered me to find the worst. Again I bought tongues because tongues have uttered some of the greatest lies!"

Is there any way to control the tongue? Are we left helpless, like a ship without a rudder or a rider on a wild horse?

Solomon wrote: "Commit thy works unto the Lord, and thy thoughts shall be established" (Proverbs 16:3). Commit your heart to the Lord and your tongue is committed. If the heart belongs to the Lord, it becomes a rudder for the tongue. The secret of tongue control is to look to the Captain of life, Jesus Christ.

There was a terrific storm, which struck fear into the hearts of passengers and sailors alike. One sailor ventured up to the deck to see the captain. The angry waves crashed over the deck nearly washing the sailor overboard. Finally he reached the captain who was standing straight and tall with his hands firmly on the wheel, staring into the face of the storm. Confidence emanated from his face. The sailor returned to the crew. "Have no fear," he said, "I have seen the captain's face. We will make it!"

We need to look to Jesus for help. The inconsistency vanishes with His help. In Exodus 15, Moses and the Israelites came to a water hole called Marah, which means bitterness. The people could not drink and murmured against Moses. The Lord directed Moses to throw a tree into the bitter water. Moses obeyed. The water became sweet and suitable for drink. The bitterness of life is erased when we look to the tree of

Calvary. There we see an empty tree. Christ died and arose from the grave to set us free. With His help even our tongues cease their clamoring and clacking.

DISCUSSION-STARTER QUESTIONS

1. Why is the tongue like a mirror?

2. Why can't careless remarks be taken back?

3. Is there any way to control the tongue? If so, how?

4. Why is the tongue so inconsistent?

5. Do we ever gain complete mastery over the tongue?

6. How does the Lord take this weak member, the tongue, and use it for His glory?

7. What is the difference between a converted tongue and an unconverted one?

8. Why do we hear Christian tongues clamoring and clacking?

"Submit yourselves there-fore to God. Resist the devil, and he will flee from you." (James 4:7)

PATTERN 10   CUTTING THE UMBILICAL CORD

At the age of two my son had an operation for a navel hernia. Naturally he had fears about going to the hospital for an operation. To ease his mind we told him he had to get a new belly button because he had worn out the first one. This apparently calmed his fears, for it pleased him to think his belly button would look better after the operation.

My son's navel hernia was congenital. The psalmist David points out that the burden of sin is congenital (Psalm 51). The fallen Adamic nature of man is to sin, since man loves darkness more than he loves light (John 3:19). Man has lost his pathway. He no longer walks in the coolness of the evening in the garden with God; now he must find God in the heat of the day.

The garden is over, but man forever seeks to regain entrance of his own accord. He reckons the garden to be all kinds of things: position, money, fame, intellectualism, power, etc. He forgets that it is fellowship with God! The groping for what has been lost is an intense inner struggle. It's as if man is seeking to capture a mythological godlikeness.

Man is earthbound, and all his inclinations are earthy. It is difficult for him to catch and hold a heavenly vision. He is like the astronaut "walking" in space. The "walk" is limited by his oxygen "umbilical cord." The astronaut can go only so far from the ship, then he must return. Natural man's umbilical cord limits his walk. Since the castastrophic fall man wanders in vain and often trips over his own cord. Wars, lust, killings, etc., are all a result of the fall. God created everything perfect, but man soon left it out to spoil.

Strife and dissension in the body of Christ can be attributed to a reversion to the old Adamic nature. Wars and fightings within the body are due to the carnival of carnality. "Ye lust, and have not: ye kill, and desire to have, and cannot obtain: ye fight and war, yet ye have not, because ye ask not" (4:2). James is using very strong language here. Did any of those early Christians actually kill? Keep in mind the words of our Lord: "Ye have heard that it was said by them of old time, Thou shalt not kill; and whosever shall kill shall be in danger of the judgment: but I say unto you, That whosoever is angry with his brother without a cause shall be in danger of the judgment" (Matthew 5:21, 22).

In my opinion, the killing that James refers to in his letter is strife in the fellowship. The concerned community was upset by believers who became jealous of one another. Any jealousy is the beginning of dislike. Dislike in its final stage is hatred! It's always the case that whenever jealousy is allowed to grow, it ends up in disappointment and grief. You cannot obtain because of such carnality.

Consider the anatomy of the body, which can be symbolic of the body of Christ. In a well-functioning body each member is important. Cooperation is most essential in the body. When my legs move, they cooperate perfectly in order to carry me from one place to another. To get out of step might possibly cause me to fall. Now, if strife enters the body there is real trouble. Suppose my elbow suddenly wants to become a knee. Do you think my elbow could function as a knee?

Suppose my thumb wants to become a nose. It would like to breathe, sneeze, and snore as a nose does. Do you think a thumb could ever become a nose? Not in a thousand years of a natural lifetime could a thumb become a nose. The thumb must recognize its gifts as a thumb and remain in the body as a thumb. Modern surgery possibly could transplant my thumb to another body, as a thumb, but never as a nose. Once a thumb always a thumb! To be transplanted as a nose would destroy its function, and be detrimental to the entire body. In other words, a thumb can never obtain as a nose, even if it wanted to. Whenever we strive to be something other than our calling, we fail miserably and do not obtain.

James makes a startling statement. He claims we don't have because we don't ask, and when we do ask, we ask for the wrong things. First, we don't have because we make no petitions and offer no thanksgiving. We simply do not pray! The crying need of the church today is for praying Christians. People who neglect prayer know nothing of the efficacy of prayer. Prayer is like a foreign language to them. They are undeserving of the name Christian. A Christian who doesn't pray is like an airplane pilot who never checks in with the control tower. He is taking his life in his own hands!

A prayerless believer is like an individual who decides not to use one of his arms. He looks at his arms and decides he doesn't need two. He ties one behind him. What happens to that unused arm? It becomes listless and weak. The same thing happens to prayerless Christians. They wither on the vine.

Second, James states: "Ye ask, and receive not, because ye ask amiss" (4:3). Although it appears that James is speaking in paradoxical riddles, he is not. Some people do not pray, and consequently there is strife. Others pray and miss the mark because they pray from a carnal base. They have ignored a grand principle, which I call the principle of utilitarianism. Philosophers stress a utilitarian principle as doing that which brings the greatest good to the greatest number. That isn't the principle here. James has discovered God's utilitarian principle. It is this: Do all you can for God's interest, and you will interest people in God. Seek first the kingdom of God, and you will be useful to Him in winning others.

Some of those early believers had missed that principle and missed the mark in their prayers. They were walking in the flesh and not in the Spirit. The same thing happened in Corinth. Believers were putting their umbilical cords back on and reverting to the flesh (old nature). Worldly investments had gotten them so involved that they had little time for the Lord. A carnal person vacillates back and forth like a pendulum. He wants Jesus as Savior, but not as Lord. He hasn't submitted his life because he loves the world too much.

Strife handicaps the body of Christ. We are vessels to be filled with the Holy Spirit. In any tense situation or division in the church, it is because the believer has allowed the flesh (old nature) to take over for a spell. The Holy Spirit's role has been relegated to that of an observer and not a controller! The Holy Spirit never argues with himself. Our spirits do the arguing. James says: "The spirit that dwelleth in us lusteth to envy" (4:5).

The principle of utilitarianism can be applied to our lives by submission to Him. Submission to God's will brings usefulness to His glory. "Submit yourselves therefore to God" (4:7). To submit to God is to resist the devil. Submission brings a cleansing of one's hands or works, and a purifying of one's heart or thoughts.

Submission is an act of faith. With faith, the umbilical cord of worldliness is severed. The announcement is: Welcome to the new world!

DISCUSSION-STARTER QUESTIONS

1. What is natural man's umbilical cord?

2. What is carnality?

3. Is a carnal person a saved person?

4. Is it possible for a true believer to drift into carnality? If so, how?

5. How do we know whether or not we have submitted to God?

6. What is the best way, or means, of avoiding carnality?

"Ye have lived in pleasure on the earth, and been wanton; ye have nourished your hearts, as in a day of slaughter. Ye have condemned and killed the just; and he doth not resist you." (James 5:5, 6)

PATTERN 11   THE GREEN CALF

When Moses delayed in coming down from Mount Sinai, the people grew restless. They went to Aaron for leadership. Aaron proved incapable of leading God's people, for he led them into idolatry. He fashioned a molten calf for worship and proclaimed a day of feasting (Exodus 32:2-5). God was greatly displeased over this because they had broken the first Commandment: "Thou shalt have no other gods before me" (Exodus 20:3).

Today we live in a materialistic-minded society. The golden calf has become the green calf. Much energy and intelligence is spent in fashioning this calf. Jesus said: "No man can serve two masters: for either he will hate the one, and love the other; or else he will hold to the one, and despise the other. Ye cannot serve God and mammon" (Matthew 6:24). Someone has said, "Money is a good servant, but a bad master!"

James echoes severe warning for the rich in

this chapter: "Your gold and silver is cankered; and the rust of them shall be a witness against you" (5:3). The issue before us is not money itself, but how we obtain our money and what we do with it. People are mistaken when they say, "Money is the root of all evil." Not so! Money is used to build hospitals, churches, schools, homes, and seminaries. Money is used to send missionaries all over the world. It takes money to run God's program. "The love of money is the root of all evil," according to 1 Timothy 6:10. We break God's law when we begin to worship this green calf.

James issues a clear warning to those who have gotten gain at the expense of others. The cries of those poor laborers who have been mistreated and underpaid, or even misled by fraud, have gone up before the Lord. Listen to this rendering from *The New International Version:* "Your gold and silver are corroded. Their corrosion will testify against you and eat your flesh like fire. You have hoarded wealth in the last days. Look! The wages you failed to pay the workmen who mowed your fields are crying out against you. The cries of the harvesters have reached the ears of the Lord All-powerful" (5:3, 4). God was the counsel for these poor laborers. James is urging them to be patient and to trust God. "Cast all your anxiety on him because he cares for you" (1 Peter 5:7, *The New International Version*). We may not possess the material resources to fight the Goliaths of wealth, but that should never diminish our faith. God is faithful to His own children. If God wants Goliath brought down, He can do it!

There was a man who had a new automobile that caught fire and was a total loss. He asked for damages against the automobile company that manufactured his car. They refused, claiming it was impossible for the car to catch on fire as he explained. A court battle followed.

The automobile company sent two of their experts to the courtroom in their defense. They presented their case with drawings and electronic equipment. A complete simulated dashboard of the automobile in question was exhibited and explained with regard to the wiring. They knew what they were talking about; they had never lost a case in court.

The decision went to the jury. After deliberating for some time, they reached a verdict. The jury found the automobile company at fault and awarded damages to the man. The automotive experts were furious. They went to some of the jurors and asked how they reached this verdict. It was pointed out that all felt the case was airtight, except for one woman. "She changed our minds," the jurors said.

These experts were baffled. One woman changed the mind of eleven jurors? Impossible! They went to the woman as she was leaving the courtroom.

"Lady, what makes you so sure we were wrong?" they asked.

"Oh, it was easy," she replied. "I listened to the jurors debating for an hour, and then they asked my opinion. I told them exactly how the fire started. You see, about a year ago the same thing happened to my car, only we managed to put the fire out and to correct the faulty wiring."

"Show us," the two men insisted. The lady took their simulated dashboard with its wires and pointed out exactly how the fire began. The two men were amazed and said, "That's right. That's how it started!"

Needless to say, the woman was surprised at this statement. "You mean, you knew all along and didn't tell, in fact, tried to prove it was impossible?"

"Yes," they said. "Our job is to defend the company. This is the first case we've lost, and we lost it because of your knowledge of the truth!"

Most of us are not so fortunate as the man who won his case. The goliaths of our society have too much money and power. Someone has said, "When money speaks, truth keeps silent." James is aware of this, but he urges the Christians to be patient and to trust God. "Vengeance is mine; I will repay, saith the Lord" (Romans 12:19).

In this country a man is protected by warranties, insurance, and certain rights of the consumer. The Christian should not be bent on making an easy dollar from every bad experience. People will sue today at the drop of a hat. Christians should be able to settle their disputes without going to court. Remember, the Holy Spirit doesn't strive against the Holy Spirit.

A church member recently sued a preacher. It seems the preacher had promised blessings if the man began tithing. The man tithed, and when no blessings came, he sued. He couldn't sue God, so he sued God's representative. The case is still pending. It's evident the man gave his tithe with a selfish motive, thus missing any possible future blessings. It's also possible that the preacher misled the man.

James says that the greed for wealth makes one fat for the slaughter. Materialism has become a god of our society. People believe that if you have money, you can do anything. Isn't it ironic that on the back of a dollar bill are the words: "In God we trust"! I wonder how many people actually handle a dollar bill in its lifetime? The banker tells me that the lifetime of a dollar bill is approximately six months. For enough dollar bills, people will wander in the wilderness for forty years or more! Following the green calf will never get you into the promised land.

The dollar bill goes everywhere, back and forth across our land. It's offered to the gods of lust, pleasure, and greed. It keeps moving, unless some hoarder sticks it under a mattress. It's invested in companies and men. It's used to build bombs and political machines. It's even used to build the kingdom of God as it goes in and out of the offering plate. Money isn't evil, but the perverted use of it—that is what James attacks.

The people once brought a coin to Jesus. It was a Roman denarius worth about seventeen cents. Jesus asked: "Whose is this image and superscription?" (Matthew 22:20). On one side was the reigning emperor, Tiberius. On the other side was a superscription, the appellation or title of the emperor.

"Caesar," they nodded in approval.

"Render therefore unto Caesar the things

which are Caesar's; and unto God the things that are God's," commanded Jesus (Matthew 22:21).

Money is used to maintain governments, so taxes must be collected. Money is also used to build and maintain God's kingdom until He comes in all His glory. Then money will be laid aside in favor of the new economic system of grace and love. Until then, we must trust God and be good stewards of all we have. Ultimately every soul shall stand as a worthy or unworthy steward before God. The image and superscription may be marred and tarnished, but we know that "As we have borne the image of the earthly, we shall also bear the image of the heavenly" (1 Corinthians 15:49).

DISCUSSION-STARTER QUESTIONS

1. Do you agree that the golden calf of Americans is the green calf?

2. Is it wrong to be rich? Can you be a Christian and be wealthy?

3. Is it realistic to think that Christians can settle their disputes without going to court?

4. Can God use a prostitute's money or a gambler's money? What does God really want?

5. Do you think Christians should "render unto Caesar," even if a large portion of it goes into war machines? What would Jesus say?

6. Should we expect blessings from our giving to Him?

> "Be patient therefore, brethren, unto the coming of the Lord. Behold, the husbandman waiteth for the precious fruit of the earth, and hath long patience for it, until he receive the early and latter rain. Be ye also patient; stablish your hearts: for the coming of the Lord draweth nigh." (James 5:7, 8)

PATTERN 12   THE JOB PRINCIPLE

One of the problems that persists with us, whether we are Christian or not, is the problem of impatience. Once a woman with eight young children boarded a comfortably filled streetcar. The conductor became a trifle impatient as he waited for the family to get on board. As the mother reached the top step, the conductor asked in a sarcastic manner, "Are these all your children, Madam, or is it a picnic?"

"They are all my children," replied the mother with a grim smile, "and I assure you, it's no picnic!"

I recently heard someone say that the problem with Americans is impatience. Our state of patience is very quickly exhausted. I remember being caught in a traffic jam at the San Francisco Bay Bridge. The day was hot; radiators and people began to boil while horns honked. And despite a popular bumper sticker suggestion, they weren't honking because they loved Jesus!

Novels are shorter today because we don't have the patience to read a *Gone With the Wind.* Paperbacks are the thing. I believe *Jonathan Livingston Seagull* was such a success partly because it could be read in such a short time. We are so pressed for time that we've blown holes in our mufflers of patience.

James wants us to have a persevering patience. "Ye have heard of the patience of Job" (5:11). Job was a very wealthy and godly man. He was one of the outstanding patriarchs of the ancient world. He was a man of prestige, for God had blessed him. Suddenly things fell apart.

In this world we cannot guarantee that anything will remain the same for long. Time has a way of changing things. We know, by reading the book of Job, that Satan was given permission to test Job. He could do just about anything but kill Job. He certainly tried to kill Job's faith! Disaster struck with the force of a flood. Job was destroyed financially. Death hit the family. Job himself was afflicted with boils from head to foot.

Job had a difficult time understanding why God allowed these things to happen. He had always served God, so why should he suffer? We ask the same question. So did the Christians in James's day. Let us not forget: "The trying of your faith worketh patience" (1:3). Job saw in the end "that the Lord is very pitiful, and of tender mercy" (5:11). God doesn't forget us in our trials.

When we analyze the patience of Job, we discover an amazing principle. Faith is patience expressed eschatologically. Putting it very simply it is: Faith is patience framed in hope. Job survived because his patience rested in faith and in hope, not on himself or his friends. "I know that my redeemer liveth, and that he shall stand at the latter day upon the earth" (Job 19:25). This principle, which I call the Job principle, runs throughout the letter of James. The principle does not contradict the definition of faith given in Hebrews, but rather corroborates it. There we read: "Faith is the substance of things hoped for, the evidence of things not seen" (Hebrews 11:1). Faith rests upon and in Jesus, and in the great doctrine of His coming again. My faith in Jesus gives me salvation, and I live in hope of His coming. Until He comes, I must patiently endure! That's why James said: "Be patient therefore, brethren, unto the coming of the Lord" (5:7).

The object of our faith is in Jesus and in the hope of His coming. The object of Job's faith was in God and in God's promises. We discover this principle at work in James's advice to those early Christians. In pattern 11 we saw them at the mercy of wealthy landowners. Consider what *The New International Version* says: "Look! The wages you failed to pay the workmen who mowed your fields are crying out against you. The cries of the harvesters have reached the ears of the Lord All-powerful. You have lived on earth in luxury and self-indulgence. You have fattened yourselves in the day of slaughter. You have condemned and murdered innocent men, who were not opposing you" (5:4-6).

As I see the picture, wealthy landowners were hiring the people to reap their fields and then withholding some of their pay. The withholdings were not taxes, but fraudulent acts on the part of the landowners. The poor people had no way to combat this. They had to work, and some money was better than none. They weren't unionized and couldn't go on strike. If they refused to work, others would merely take their place. Many of these poor people were Christians and James was concerned for them.

No doubt, some were threatening violence, to get even with the rich by burning their fields and barns. However, if they put the rich out of business by burning their fields, then everyone would be out of work. Bitterness and hatred were building up in their minds. They were caught in an economic vise, and their patience was virtually exhausted. James castigates the rich for pilfering the poor. He booms out: "Ye have condemned and killed the just; and he doth not resist you" (5:6). James realizes that many of these Christians had reached a boiling point.

Is it any different today? It's certainly more complicated, but the issues are similar. Today we have unions pressing the employers for more pay, and the employers pressing the employees for more production. The results of such stalemates are: lettuce boycotts, table grape boycotts, automobile workers' strikes; telephone workers' strikes, steel workers' strikes, railroad shutdowns, airline workers' strikes, and so on. After all is said and done, who really comes out on top?

In each of us there is a patience point where we just can't take any more. James exhorts us to allow God to soothe our wounds and mold our patience. "Behold, we count them happy which endure" (5:11), writes James. He reminds us all of the patience of Job. That's the kind of patience necessary to meet the storms of life. They had seen the end of the Lord. Some might even have witnessed His resurrected body. The hope of His coming plus patient endurance makes a good recipe. I remind you again: Faith is patience framed in hope!

The Hebrew children prayed for about four hundred years for a deliverer. Generation after generation lived in slavery in Egypt. Their prayers went up like heat rising from the desert sand. It was a long, hard lesson in persevering prayer, but God heard. Patience in prayer always pays dividends. The heavens are not brass. In God's time He sent Moses. The message God gave to Moses was that He had heard the cry of His people (Exodus 3:7).

When a people have hope, they will not perish. The Hebrew children had hope that God would send a deliverer. These early Christians had hope. They believed Jesus was coming back soon. They never conceived of His promise to return to be a thousand years and more in the future. The eternal hope of the Christian has always been, and always will be, Christ is coming!

This very hope should be sufficient to increase patience to its maximum. James urges them to remember this hope in the face of adversity. As the farmer plants his crops and waits for the rains, so must the Christian work in expectancy of Christ. James tells them to establish their hearts, to be fortified with this blessed hope, and to cement this hope in their hearts!

Finally he writes: "Don't grumble against each other, brothers, or you will be judged. The Judge is standing at the door!" (5:9, *The New International Version*). In other words, the Judge is about to come out of His chambers to open the case. Take heart. Justice is coming. There was a song a few years ago that had a delightful and encouraging chorus, "You gotta have heart . . ."

Job discovered what everyone must do in the midst of trial. The psalmist says it right: "Wait on the Lord: be of good courage, and he shall strengthen thine heart: wait, I say, on the Lord" (Psalm 27:14).

If we withdraw into the hole of self-pity, we will find a bottomless pit. Job sat on a pile of ashes picking at his sores and contemplating his misery. It just got worse each day. Nothing changed for the better until he began to pray for his friends. The very day he began to look away from himself and to pray for his friends was the very day God acted to heal him. When he looked to God for his friends, God looked to him.

Things may appear hopeless, but God is good. Remember, faith is patience framed in hope.

DISCUSSION-STARTER QUESTIONS

1. What is meant by the principle that faith is patience framed in hope?

2. What do you think Job meant by the statement: "I know that my redeemer liveth, and that he shall stand at the latter day upon the earth" (Job 19:25)?

3. What is faith? What is patience? What is hope?

4. How can one wait on the Lord? Does this mean to do nothing?

5. What changed Job's circumstances?

6. How can the hope of Christ coming in the future help us in the problems of today?

"Is any sick among you? let him call for the elders of the church; and let them pray over him, anointing him with oil in the name of the Lord: and the prayer of faith shall save the sick, and the Lord shall raise him up; and if he have committed sins, they shall be forgiven him."
(James 5:14, 15)

PATTERN 13   THE PETER PRINCIPLE

In the introductory statements of *The Peter Principle,* Raymond Hull raises some very serious questions pertaining to incompetence and why things always go wrong. The formula proposed in *The Peter Principle* is very simply stated: "In a hierarchy every employee tends to rise to his level of incompetence."*

Mr. Hull points out that the term hierarchy was originally used to describe the graduated, or ranking system of the priesthood. It is suggested that in every hierarchy, even in the church, employees are promoted to a "level of incompetence."

As I read this fascinating best-seller, I asked myself, "Does this really apply to the church?" Is it true that pastors, and other workers of the various ministries, reach a level of incompetence?

---

*Laurence J. Peter & Raymond Hull, *The Peter Principle* (New York: William Morrow & Co., Inc., 1969), p. 25.

Most of God's workers are volunteers. The job of the believers' church is to try to bring this priesthood of believers into a competent ministry. Are we succeeding?

Think about it! What is the main concern of your church? Is it the budget, the building program, or how much you're paying the preacher? What does the pastor find himself doing with the majority of his time? If he's a typical pastor he envisions workers going out into the fields ripe unto harvest. However, just the contrary happens. No one goes out but the pastor, and most of his calls are, of necessity, confined to the membership.

And what about this priesthood of believers? Are they content that the church is functioning on a level of such incompetence? It isn't enough just to meet the church budget, or to have a well-liked man fill the pulpit, or to maintain a comfortable, air-conditioned building. Somehow this smacks of incompetent service! I believe God expects other priorities from this priesthood of believers.

Paul writes: "It was he who gave some to be apostles, some to be prophets, some to be evangelists, and some to be pastors and teachers, to prepare God's people for works of service, so that the body of Christ may be built up" (Ephesians 4:11, 12, *The New International Version*).

God equips people with gifts to reach other people. The true ministry of the church is building Christ in people. This is how the body grows. Someone has said, "God doesn't care so much about the work as He does the worker!" We reach a level of incompetence and hindrance when we put buildings and programs above the needs of God's people. What good is a $500,000 air-conditioned sanctuary if the people aren't trusting the Lord and discovering that He supplies all our daily needs? Does God want an air-conditioned monument or a living body?

In Exodus 2:21 we read: "And Moses was content to dwell with the man." At that point Moses had reached a plateau of service. God would call him into new life. The fire of the burning bush would be symbolic of the new fire ignited in his soul! The vision of the burning bush kept Moses going throughout his long, arduous ministry. The church needs this burning-bush vision today.

James sensed the need for the vision in his day. He saw that the trials and pressures of society have a way of killing enthusiasm for the Lord. The awful monotony of life is apt to quench the fires of faith. The hope of His coming is forgotten in the cauldron of sickness or discouragement. Time has a way of making one weary in well-doing. No one likes to row upstream every day of his life. James calls the colony of believers to act as believers possessing new life. He urges them to put on the blue jeans of works and to make their faith come alive for Christ.

"Is any sick among you? let him call for the elders of the church; and let them pray over him, anointing him with oil in the name of the Lord" (5:14). "Cast all your anxiety on him because he cares for you" (1 Peter 5:7, *The New Interna-*

tional Version). The kingdom of God means rolling up our sleeves and working.

In Acts we read that Peter was confined in prison. "Prayer was made without ceasing of the church unto God for him" (Acts 12:5). The early believers called upon God to deliver Peter. God answered in a dramatic way. Peter was miraculously delivered. It was such a miracle that Peter couldn't believe it. He thought he was dreaming, but soon discovered that nothing was beyond the power of God. He went to the house of Mary, where the people were praying. He knocked and a girl named Rhoda answered. She was so surprised to see Peter that she left him standing at the door!

She ran in and interrupted the prayer meeting. An amazing thing had happened, but they didn't believe her! "She's out of her mind," they said. "Peter's in jail, and we're praying for him!" The record shows that Peter continued knocking. I believe Peter pounded on the door to get their attention.

What was wrong with that prayer meeting? The same thing that is sometimes wrong today. We don't believe in the power of God. We don't anticipate God's help. We aren't really expecting supernatural intervention. James urges them to anoint and to pray expecting something to happen. God delights to work in the dynamic of positive expectancy. What a delight it is to those who are expecting something.

But understand the order of God's actions. James was speaking to and about Christians —the saved. First let's get that straight. God is mainly interested in our salvation. The soul is of prime importance, not the body. But He is interested and will take an interest in our well-being. Paul prayed for deliverance from a thorn in the flesh. Instead of physical deliverance, he received grace. Grace flooded his soul like sunshine through a stained glass window. In the providence of God some are raised up and healed physically, whereas others receive sufficient grace. In both cases there is healing! Often physical healing is a direct result of spiritual healing.

I once visited a dear saint who was in intensive care due to a coronary. She was in critical condition. We committed her to the Lord according to this passage—anointing and all. I wasn't sure of God's will for her future, but I was sure of His interest in her. She recovered! Later she confided to me that after the anointing she felt the presence of the Holy Spirit. This testimony came from one not given to emotional tangents; I have no reason to question her integrity.

I am convinced that much healing in the church would take place if we would confess our sins to God. There are also times we need to confess our faults one to another (5:16). We cannot expect the refreshing flow of the Holy Spirit in our lives if He is dammed up by sin. When He is released, we are released.

In the Presence of Mine Enemies, by Jeremia Denton, we read of his POW experiences in North Vietnam. He was tortured and thrown into solitary confinement. They put clamps on him and tightened them which produced excruciating pain. At one point Denton said he could take no more and prayed for help. He had reached maximum human endurance. It was at this point that God gave Him comforting presence. Denton felt the assurance of God's presence, and his pain vanished. He said they returned to tighten the clamps, but the more they tightened them, the more comfortable he felt! God had enveloped him in His loving care.

The same Presence that had opened Peter's jail cell also breached the prison walls of North Vietnam and an intensive care unit in Stockton, California. The only difference was a time span of nearly two thousand years! What a marvelous God we have!

God raises us from the depths of incompetence to the heights of service. Without Him we excuse ourselves as inferior saints—and we are! The Peter Principle for indolent saints is: In church every saint is tempted to rest in a level of incompetence.

It's almost an afterthought that James throws in Elijah as an example. Elijah was ordinary, with one exception. This exception made him extraordinary. He prayed, expecting God to do something. He wasn't content to be an ordinary member of God's organization. He had the kind of faith that turned a cloud the size of a man's hand into a ferocious storm. Miraculous? You bet!

Blue jeans faith is always miraculous because it works. Put it on and see. You'll never be the same. But watch out, you're in for some God-filled surprises.

DISCUSSION-STARTER QUESTIONS

1. Do you think the Peter Principle applies to the church?

2. How does God overcome the Peter Principle in His work?

3. What is the main concern of your church? Is it equipping people for the work of the ministry?

4. How does one maintain a burning-bush vision?

5. Do you agree that every saint is tempted to rest in a level of incompetence?

6. Do you think we pray with expectancy?